SARAH BICKFORD

Sarah Bickford
as a young woman
Courtesy of Sheridan Public
Sheridan, Montana

Sarah Bickford

"From Rags To Riches"

Few stories of the Old West and of women of the Old West particularly are more fascinating than that of Sarah Bickford, especially in the light of so many today who seem to bemoan the status of being black. Sarah was a black woman who lived in one of Montana's earliest towns, Virginia City, and made good for herself, like few women of that time ever did. She did this in a time when many women had come to the West to sell their bodies and probably did little more than that. She had dignity and respect, and towards the end of her life — she had quite a bit of money!

What is more amazing about Sarah Bickford is that she started her life as a slave in the South. Here is the story of Sarah, and how she went from rags to riches. Her story is inspiring, not just for blacks, but for all of us.

In other literature about women of the old West, it has been said that women were responsible for "taming" the wild West, and establishing many civilized things that made our world sane. But it is also true that many women were destructive, and because of them society and culture were corrupted. Many women seeking fortune could only seek selling their bodies and their souls. About Sarah Bickford we know that her aspirations were much higher. She was obviously a woman of worth, and this fact seems to not have been lost on the men of her day. She courageously left her first marriage where she was being abused, and found a highly respectable man after that, a man of means that married her. Sarah is a woman who did help to tame the wild West. She brought integrity and strength to Montana.

Someone said, seeing her photo, that she was probably an attractive woman and this was one of the reasons she caught the attention of the men who eventually married her, and this may be true, but she was more than a pretty face.

Some Washington State University students, interested in researching African Americans in places in America where they have been overlooked, particularly in the West, did research on Sarah's life. This research has contributed a lot to my knowledge of her. Sarah Gammon Bickford was born on Christmas Day in 1852, in North Carolina or Tennessee, as the slave of a prominent citizen, John Blair III. Jonesboro is the oldest community in Tennessee with a rich history and highly preserved historic downtown.

Sarah was listed in an 1860 census for slaves as an eight-year-old female, mulatto slave. Yes, mulattos, and anyone with a mix of races, whether it be European and Black, European and Eskimo, or Asian and Native American for examples, is often very attractive. Nature seems to favor the mixing of the races. So, Sarah could well have been a very attractive woman.

John Blair and his two brothers, William and Robert, were already quite wealthy, but then went on to strike it even richer in the 1849 California gold rush. All three returned from the gold fields to Tennessee with enough backing capital to invest in businesses and build life-long financial security. John Blair, who was the owner of Sarah's parents, died in 1863. Sarah Bickford's children orally passed down her family history. What they told indicates that Sarah's parents were sold during the Civil War, after which she never saw them again. In the settlement of Blair's vast estate upon his death, Sarah's parents could have been taken from her because they were "property" that was sold off.

During the Civil War, eastern Tennessee was sympathetic to the Union and so was the Blair family. Jonesboro families were mostly sympathetic to the Union. John was born in 1790. He pursued a career in law and politics, serving as a Tennessee Senator, a US Congressman, and acquired part shares in a large iron company. John and Mary, his wife, lived in a large brick country mansion built by slave labor in 1814. The home and the slave quarters adjacent to it stand as reminders of the skilled slave masons who built it. There is a good chance that Sarah was born in the adjoining slave quarters, and would have worked alongside her mother in the Blair mansion. The Blairs also owned a home and hotel in Jonesboro, and John ran the hotel. Most likely, Sarah also worked at this hotel. Sarah would have taken the name Blair after her owner. Apparently, slaves took the last name of their owners.

Nathan Gammon is another prominent Jonesboro resident who had a lot to do with Sarah's early history. He and John Blair had several business dealings in Jonesboro before he moved in 1851 or 1852, and he was also a slave owner. He had a slave named Isaac Gammon. Isaac was romantically involved with a woman who was Sarah's aunt. Her aunt was a free black woman, named Nancy Jones, later, Nancy Jones Gammon, as she took Isaac's last name even though she wasn't allowed to officially marry him until later. In 1874, Nancy testified that her mother had also been free, raising speculation as to how her mother had been free, but her mother's sister had been a slave (the sister being Sarah's mother). More research is needed to understand exactly what Sarah's relationship was to Nancy. Nancy's Isaac is described as a "giant negro" with the nickname "one-eyed Ike."

Nancy described Nathan Gammon as "kind and indulgent" because he allowed Isaac and her to have a relationship before the end of slavery and also allowed Isaac to own swine. In January 1866, as the long and bloody war came to a close, Nancy and Isaac were married. But other memories of Mr. Gammon cause us to doubt how kind and indulgent he really was. When the war was still on, Gammon said to Isaac, "If I really thought you were serious about this Union business, I would have you killed."

African American man of the 1800s

Sarah celebrated her new-found freedom after the war, freed by the Emancipation Proclamation, by moving to live with Nancy and Isaac. They were now in Knoxville, as Nathan Gammon had moved there and taken his slaves with him. Before his death in 1874, Isaac served as the first elected African American Alderman in Knoxville and as an elected police/fireman. Sarah changed her last name to Gammon after her aunt.

Sarah met John Lutrell Murphy in Knoxville sometime between 1865 and 1870. Major Murphy had commanded companies A,B, C, and D of the 60th US Regiment of Colored Infantry in Arkansas. Soon after the War he moved to Knoxville and obtained a license to practice law in August of 1867, He was married to a woman named Viola, but she stayed in Knoxville while John moved to Montana, taking his two foster children, and Sarah as a nanny in 1871. Sarah's trip west was the payment for her services as a nanny. He only stayed in Montana for a short time. Sarah stayed in Montana and her footprint on Montana's history is indelible. But here is where we need to make a contrast between how Sarah came

to Montana, and how so many other young

The cover of a 1918 issue of the Ladies Home Journal is found intact in a layer of wall events

women of her day came to Montana.

This was during the gold rush years, and because there were so many men coming to the wild west seeking their fortune in gold, there were also plenty of women seeking their fortune in the men who were seeking their fortune. I understand now that people are and were the same then as they are today. We always see people in "the old days" in such a rosy light and always assume that they were so saintly. This of course does not refer to days as old as Sodom and Gomorrah, mind you, but just days past, maybe a hundred, maybe two hundred years ago. But what was happening in the wild West, and certain key figures of that time help to show that people were the same, essentially as they are now. The wild West was the WILD West. Prostitution had gone hog-wild. Butte had been dubbed "the sink-hole of America" because it had only about 100,000 people living in it, yet it had thousands of prostitutes roaming its streets. Butte was a wild city. And so we can assume that there were plenty of women who had set their sites on simply coming to the West and selling their bodies to the men of the West. Sarah had much higher standards for herself, during this same era. She had been a slave, she of all people could think of herself as deserving no better than to sell her body in the West.

There are books by a bizarre woman named Mary Maclane who had come to Butte by means of her mother who had brought her in her teens, but she ended up being a highly influential figure in her day. Around 1900 she was writing books that were bestsellers, and she even caught Ernest Hemingway's attention. One of her bestsellers, her autobiography, describes what a tortured soul she is, how she wishes she could be happy, but there is no hope. And she seems to have sold her soul to the devil and talks about how she loves the devil even though he offers her no hope and no happiness. She had a "crush" on an older woman who had been her teacher. It was one of the most bizarre books I have ever read, yet it shows how people were bizarre then too. Apparently, many people were greatly influenced by her beliefs, or lack thereof. I heard that this woman had also become a prostitute in Butte. But Sarah! She was a person of hope, courage, strength and purpose. In her quiet corner, she was slaying dragons.

Another way in which people are no different yesterday than they are today is in this thing of prostitution cropping up around a "gold rush." Today, the same problem arose in North Dakota when their "oil rush" took place. Suddenly, they were having a prostitution problem. People are just the same. Sarah is a strong and courageous figure in the midst of it all.

Virginia City was like so many towns in Montana in the mid to late 1800s. The main draw was the gold rush, plus there were gems to be found in Montana, and in Butte, copper was also being mined. Today, Montana is called "The Treasure State." Virginia City and Nevada City, right next door to Virginia City are now just ghost towns. Both are used for tourism. Bannack, another city about 60 miles away, is also just a ghost town used for tourism, though it was a thriving town in the 1800s. Bannack was also the capital of Montana but this was later moved to Helena. The old rustic buildings are mostly the originals, though there were more than exist today. Each has a story. Some are a little spooky and seem haunted. But these towns cropped up during this important era.

John Murphy went to Virginia City because he received an appointment as a territorial judge. His wife didn't want to go, perhaps because it was not meant to be a permanent move, and

Civil War African American Soldier

African American men of the 1800s in the West

Sarah probably gave her every confidence that she would just do her job as a nanny and not interfere in any way with the relationship.

In Knoxville and throughout much of her later life in Montana, Sarah Gammon worked as a domestic servant. Upon her arrival in Virginia City, Sarah was employed as a chambermaid at the Madison House Hotel on Wallace Street across from, and one block east of the Territorial Capitol Building. In Virginia City, Sarah met one of the miners who had come to this part of the world, and she got married. She didn't sell her body, she made him "buy the cow!" He was a black man named John L. Brown. She and John had three children William, Leonard and Eva. In 1879, both of her sons died from a diphtheria epidemic, and three years later, Eva died. In addition to this, her husband was abusing her to the point that she sought divorce!

Her life and her story is one of great struggle. For the second time in her life she suffered the loss of her entire immediate family! Oral tradition states that Sarah kept a picture of Eva in her bedroom until the day she died.

In November of 1880 she sued John for divorce. Now here again, she stands out against the women of her day. While there were women in Butte, accepting the degradation of a single "crib" for their profession and possibly a pimp who forced them to "perform" an unbelievable number of acts per day, Sarah was defying society, which would frown on a woman getting a divorce, and saying that she was worthy of more than the abuse that this man was giving her. In making her private trauma public and risking the stigma of divorce, she sought to protect her remaining child, seven-year-old Eva.

Sarah's testimony in her divorce case states: "That since marriage up to and until the abandonment and desertion hereinafter set forth — to with on the 15th day of April 1879 – the defendant did treat this plaintiff in a cruel and inhuman manner. . ." Brown beat Sarah with his fists and wooden broom, and threatened her life with both a knife and revolver. She was granted a divorce in November 1880 and was given sole custody of

Eva, the surviving child of the marriage. In 1882, nine-year-old Eva died of pneumonia. This was not an unusual story at a time when one in every five children died before the age of five, but it was nonetheless heartbreaking to the mother.

Again a free woman, Sarah went to work in the French Canadian household of Adaline Laurin. Soon after the ever resourceful Sarah opened a bakery, restaurant, and lodging house on Wallace Street in downtown Virginia City, perhaps with Laurin's financial assistance. The bakery took in boarders, offering "Meals and Lunches at all hours, Fresh bread, Cakes, Pies and Confectionary Constantly At Hand," so stated the advertisement in the Madisonian in 1880 and 1881. Bickford's business endeavors demonstrate the value of traditional women's work in Montana Territory's primarily male mining camps.

In 1883, Sarah married again, this time to a better man, better because history shows he respected her in a way her previous husband had not. She progressed. She had high hopes. She had survived many things and she didn't give up. When she had lost everything, she then started over. This time she married a prominent white man of means. 1883 was prior to Montana's 1909 Miscegenation law prohibiting interracial marriage. She had impressed a man of high standing. His name was Stephen Bickford, a farmer and miner from Maine who had moved to Montana Territory in the gold rush of the 1860s.

They began life in a home Sarah owned from her previous marriage just a few miles from Virginia City. Somehow I am quite sure this was frowned on by a Christian society. Sarah then proceeded to have four more children, Elmer, Harriet, Helena and Mabel. In addition to this, she operated the New City Bakery on Wallace Street. You can see how progressive their relationship was for this era. This flies in the face of the idea that women have been kept from making a good living, on their own, by men in America. This was already being done in the Victorian period. Women, like blacks have partly been victims of their own "victim" mentality.

In 1888, the couple moved to a home on a large piece of property East of Virginia City. It is now known as the Bickford House or Romeo

Gardens and is currently owned by the Montana Heritage Commission. In 1888, Stephen Bickford made a business decision that would ultimately change Sarah's life. He bought two-thirds share in the company that supplies Virginia City with its water. Sarah kept the books for the water company, and the previous owner also had operated a large truck garden. So she now operated the truck garden, selling produce and poultry to the surrounding community. Sarah had enormous energy. Stephen Bickford also owned various lots, mining claims, and a small farm on the East end of town where the couple lived.

Sadly, Sarah lost Stephen as well. He died March 22,1990 of pneumonia. She continued to be unstoppable. She then proceeded to buy out the remaining third share of the water company, as she had inherited his share of the water company in his $9500.00 estate. This made her the sole owner of the Virginia City Water Company, an amazing achievement for any woman in 1900, let alone an African American woman. By 1920, she had replaced a number of the deteriorating wooden pipes that provided water to local residents. Sarah Bickford not only managed the business, she personally visited every customer and learned their needs. Sarah acquired the nickname "Sallie" in Virginia City. She was also her own bill collector, keeping after her customers to pay their bills on time. She earned the respect of the community, but may not have been so popular with some.

Late in 1917, Bickford raised water rates 10 percent. The rate increase incensed her customers, who had been paying the old rate for forty years. With Prohibition about to claim his livelihood, longtime saloonkeeper Frank McKeen protested, "Here the state of Montana goes dry, and Sallie Bickford boosts the price of water. It is getting to be a hard world in which to live." But business is business, fair is fair, and Bickford did what she had to do.

After Stephen's death, Sarah had further honed her business skills through a correspondence course at a school in Scranton, Pennsylvania. In addition to buying out the water company, Sarah bought the notorious "Hangman's Building" as the Water Company's headquarters, so named because on January 14, 1863, five alleged road agents were hanged on a beam in the unfinished building by local Vigilantes. In another bold move, Sarah installed a rest room in the building for the comfort of affluent female travelers passing through town on their way to Yellowstone National Park. She also cut a trapdoor in the ceiling of the building, and for a small fee revealed the hanging beam in the Hangman's Building to curious visitors. Her son Elmer performed the day-to-day maintenance and upgrades on the water system. When she died in 1931, the Madisonian expressed the community's sadness, declaring that Virginia City had lost one of its most devoted mothers and loyal pioneer citizens.

Sarah offers many lessons to African Americans today. When her parents were sold and taken from her earlier in her life, she could have become bitter and resigned herself to live the rest of her life hating the white man and groveling in the dust. She did not choose this path. She must have had a good attitude towards people because she was successful in trades where she served people. She also was admired by men who would want to marry her, not just buy her for one night. Sarah understood the blessing of forgiving and loving in spite of her misfortunes. After she had been abused by John Brown, she also could have curled up to live the rest of her life bitter. She did not. She lived an even more productive life after that and went on to marry again and have several more children.

Sarah undoubtedly was an amazing woman, and one we should never forget. Montana today is very "white," just as it was then, but not a place where an African American would be shunned if he or she had a good attitude and an entrepreneurial spirit. Sarah showed how with the right attitude, it was possible to live a productive life amongst white people.

Hangman's building today, at Christmas, the advent of Sarah's birth

Sarah and Stephen Bickford

Sarah Bickford or "Sallie"

Western African American woman of the 1800s

Scenes from Virginia City in 2015

A Message of love and hope.

God revealed the star shining over Blacks. It is like the star that stood over Bethlehem that foretold of something great.

Black people need to know that the sojourning in America has been for a glorious future that God has prepared for them. I needed God to confirm this outside my little world, and then ran into a book by modern day prophet Rick Joyner. God has given him special gifts to predict things that will occur, proven by what has already occurred. His knowledge is by the spirit of God and has gone out to that part of the church that recognizes these gifts.

His little book is entitled Overcoming Racism. Here is an excerpt: "If the white race, or any other people, had suffered the same historic problems as the black race, we would be having the same problems they are having now. I have heard many white leaders actually say that we would have no inner city problems if blacks just had some ambition. What do you think slavery did to the work ethic? Such deep cultural wounds cannot be healed without the intervention of the cross."

"The black race in America was allowed to be subject to slavery for the same reason that the Lord allowed Israel to become slaves in Egypt — they have a destiny with God. When they come into this destiny, the rest of America is going to be very thankful for this great and noble people in our midst. It is the destiny of the black race to carry freedom to a new level. This will be true freedom, with the dignity and honor that God created men to have."

THE POWER FOR HEALING

"It was by the Lord's stripes that we were healed. In a sense we too, receive the authority for healing in the very place where we are wounded, once the wounds have been healed. Even when the wounds have been healed, there is sensitivity in that area that remains. Someone who has been subjected to abuse will be sensitive to others who have been abused. When someone who is subjected to abuse is truly healed, they will not only be truly free, but they will have the authority to carry healing to others with those same wounds."

"The black race is going to embrace the cross, receive healing for their wounds, and start loving white Americans with such power that we will all be set free by that love."

"The Uncle Tom of Uncle Tom's Cabin [you know how negatively black people have thought of this man] truly was a prophetic figure. In spite of all the abuse that he suffered at the hands of his 'owners,' he was freer than they were, and he was willing to use his freedom to lay down his life if that would result in his owner's salvation. The black believers in America, when they have been fully healed will bring revival and true spiritual liberty to the whole nation."

"The inner cities of America will ultimately become the inner sanctuary of God's tabernacle; the place where his glory and presence dwells. The greatest move of God that America has ever experienced will come out of the inner cities. The suburban church may have the gold, but the inner church will make them jealous with the glory. Those who are wise will take the gold that they have and use it to build a tabernacle for the Lord that is not made with hands, but with people."

I was shocked to read this. I had the same "premonitions" but thought it too bold to say as much as he has said. " Bring freedom to a new level!" Speaking of Uncle Tom, it is amazing that Black people have had the wisdom to embrace the same faith that many slave owners claimed to have, probably dishonestly.

WHAT YOU ARE

You are the ones who have been humbled. You are the people of God who have been put into the iron furnace that God talked about when He said that he would take the Israelites out of the iron furnace of Egypt (Deut. 4:20).

Blacks are not just called, they are chosen. The journey has been leading to things that eye has not seen, ear has not heard, and the heart has not conceived of.

Black people have been a greater testimony of change through Christ than most other people. You glorify God in ways that no other people on earth glorify Him. Whites who served Satan already knew of your great prophetic calling. So it will be no surprise to them, only perhaps to those who had not really seen what is within you. There is a prophecy also about Egypt, which is still to be fulfilled, and since it is in Africa and you are from Africa, it could be that this prophecy also is one of the reasons you have been targeted, because lovers of the devil rail against this prophecy coming true.

While some Blacks cringe to think of Jesus Christ as the banner for the American Negro, or of Martin Luther King being the prophet, because they feel that all has failed, you know that this is not true. You know that who you are in Christ is more precious in your journey than it has been for anyone else in America. You must also know that you are chosen, precious, singled out and created for a special purpose in America that will amaze every American and the world.

It's the African American and not the African, in particular. It's what you have become in Jesus Christ in your journey, your humiliation and travail in America that has made you the unique people that you are. Your place in God, your destiny is similar to the Jews, even to the point of once being slaves.

Don't you know that God doesn't waste our tribulations?

THE WORD 'BLACK'

Why are you called Black? We call sin black, we call dirt black, and we call night black and equate night with the darkness that one hides in to hide from sin. But I've been told that the blacker real dirt is, the richer it is for growing crops. The red river valley of the North has rich black dirt. So has southern Minnesota and northern Iowa.

I am a night person. I love the night. I love the quiet of the night, the peace of darkness that doesn't make my light-sensitive eyes strain, and the beauty of the lights that show in the sky against the backdrop of dark.

I wear black often because it is a dignified color. When I was a little girl I would walk a mile to school every day alone, and relish things in nature along the way-leaves, stones, and more than anything, the chestnut. I remember clearly how I loved the color of the chestnut. I would keep and collect chestnuts because of the beauty of the wood.

Do we look at mahogany and think of sin? Do we look at the gorgeous slick sides of a dark reddish-brown Arabian horse glistening in the sun and think of it as evil? When we open a can of coffee and look at the rich color and take in the rich aroma of coffee, which is awesomely more beautiful than the taste, do we think of human dung or of the filthiness of human hearts?

Why would the skin color of the African-based human being have any ugly connotations compared to the beauty of other things that also have rich tones created by the sun?
Lots of people through the ages have seen the African skin and thought it was beautiful. Anyone who thinks otherwise is blind,
absolutely blind and stupid. This is a beautiful color. White people want to get a tan, many times in excess. Doesn't that say enough?

Black people are a piece of art.

From my window far away, growing up in a small town with rather indifferent white people, to living in the inner city, I have watched black people everywhere and waited. I have waited for this sojourning to come to a beautiful purpose. God has shown it will someday come to be.

It can be discouraging, but a black face is still a happy thing to behold.

WHAT YOU POSSESS

You have the most incredible endurance of spirit. You have passion and energy. God gives greater burdens to the strong than to the weak. You are strong people. Oh my Lord you are strong people.

I am a musician. When I taught music, I ventured into teaching some flute students who had only classical music in their background, to play flute to a CD background of rock inspirations such as the Beatles. I also played keyboard in a jazz band recently in a central Minneapolis college. This was far more difficult than the mechanical style of classical. All rock and similar styles are rooted in blues and jazz — the creations of Blacks. It is the work of true genius. Genius has been overlooked. Not very many white people think about that, maybe because of pride or just ignorance.

It is not a myth that musical genius runs strong in the Black race. It is a great legacy. Rhythm is a beautiful heritage. The rhythm that was injected into our culture probably during civil rights, with more focus on Blacks brought with it an abundance of new musical styles and rhythm has changed forever the way we see and experience music!! Practically all styles that employ rhythm were the result of those early styles—ragtime, jazz and blues. Out of this to my surprise came pretty much all modern musical styles other than "new age" classical—rock, alternative rock, punk rock, hard rock, acid rock, country western(!), and many more, and evolved into newer black styles such as rap, hip-hop, rhythm and blues.

Being a musician I also know that math and music have a strong connection. People with musical ability have that sense of order that makes them good at math as well. Many Black people seem to excel in this area.

Your creative genius is expressed in other ways, such as your gift of inventing colloquialisms. In the 50s, sayings such as "You chicks," "You cats" were later adopted into the white youth community, but began in the black community. And I would like to say, you are just a unique people—your culture, your ways, and only ignorant idiots dislike what is new and different or different from themselves. We love variety in flowers and nature, why don't we love variety in humans? It has to be only because of ignorant arrogance.

Black people tend to be aggressive and excellent in the power of persuasion. This implies having a gift for sales. Black people tend to be flexible, hearty, resilient — able to bounce back.

What are you waiting for? You have genius, sales ability, flexibility, and endurance. Go in and take the Promised Land!

WHY HASN'T IT HAPPENED?

Black people, you don't have a passion for becoming a part of the white world, or becoming a part of their ways, for the most part. This has been an important factor in the fulfillment of the prophecy. You don't want the messed up ways of the white world, but you need an alternative to your own problems.

You know the problems. The list is long, and I don't need to spell it out. But Rick Joyner and Jesus say that you will come out of this and set an example to others — to the white race. That is awesome!

FEAR OF MAN

One of the biggest obstacles to going into the Promised Land is the fear of man. It brings a curse according to the ancient prophet Jeremiah.

Though fear of man is wrong, God understands how hard it is not to fear him. But Black people, this has got to go in order to conquer and go into the Promised Land.

The death of Martin Luther King inspired fear, but God doesn't want black leaders to die in their prime. It's not His will for us to die before we have finished our work on earth. Since this battle to emancipate the Black person is vehemently hated by the devil, we need to fight a spiritual battle to stand strong. Perhaps Martin Luther King waged too much of a political battle. This is not to say that he wasn't a true Christian or that it wasn't also a spiritual battle. This is not to say that people weren't praying or that Christians failed.

But the weapons of the Spirit are the only weapons that will win in this battle, no matter what we do on a human level. And we don't need to wait for any one person. We already have that one person — Jesus Christ.

Stand against that fear by God's spirit. It is not too late. God is watching over His word to perform it. He will perform it in you - His Black people.

FORGIVENESS

Everyone has a problem with forgiveness to some degree. It is one of our greatest obstacles to moving forward. Forgiveness must be a very difficult thing for Blacks. But bitterness has to go if you are going to possess the Promised Land. Black people actually possess an amazing ability to forgive and embrace another human being. It is called being "magnanimous."

One of the best portraits of forgiveness is the black Baptist minister who visited Jeffrey Dahmer in prison, resulting in his conversion. What kind of character would it take to be the only person visiting a man who killed and ate black men, and be Black yourself? This minister is the kind of Black person I have seen that I believe in.

So you may ask, if that is true, what has been going on in our world with people such as negative rappers, demonstrating such rage? It is because the sojourning has gone on for so long, and Black people have begun to buckle under it. The time is ripe for a breakthrough.

God usually asks us to make the first move. That move is toward forgiveness. He understands how hard it is for Black people but He cannot bless sin. Maybe your ancestors sinned. Forgive them. The heart of stone must turn to a heart of flesh. That is when we will see this prophecy fulfilled.

BELIEVING THE LIES

Stop believing the lies about you! You can do that when you stop trusting man and start trusting God. "Cursed is the man who trusts in man," says Jeremiah. You don't need to hear what people think of you when God has you in the palm of His hand and has created you for good works before the foundation of the World. What God thinks of you is what matters. His opinion is the one that matters.

SHAME

People who have been degraded take on the shame themselves. Stop the shame. Stop blaming yourself. Stop accepting shame just because someone may look at you in a certain way and it may be that they don't like your color. It may be that you imagine it, or it may not. God made you in His image. Jesus sees you as His righteousness. You were created in Christ Jesus for good works. You are the apple of His eye. You are His workmanship.

IT'S TIME.

It's time, Black people. It's time to win. It's time to go in and possess. It's time to know who you are in Christ.

In the world you have been the sad brunt of a joke and sometimes the object of scorn. But as God has it so often in His kingdom, you are the pearl inside the oyster (black pearl). You are the treasure that He has been working on for a glorious purpose. You are the fulfilling of the prophecy in Micah that says He is doing a work in our day that we would not believe if we were told.

But I know and believe, in part. I want to go to the Promised Land with you. I just want to be with the winners.

YOU CAME INTO JESUS LATE

The white race had Christianity in a whole culture in large numbers before any race on earth. We probably needed help a lot sooner!

You came late. In America, you may not realize that though Europe had Christianity all the way back to early AD (England, not long after 500A.D.) Europe was still a bastion of evil and oppression. In fact, after the introduction of Christianity, we remained pagan for many years. (Note the hypocrisy of condemning African pagan practices.) Christianity had a hard time becoming part of the culture and many Europeans continued in their pagan ways long after it was introduced.

My Swedish ancestors were sharecroppers. Most people were poor and the wealth was inherited and owned by an elite group — the upper class. Over all of Europe this was true. My ancestors as sharecroppers lived on the property of someone rich and were allowed to live in a dump and survive by working for the people on that land. They did not necessarily even eat well. The need for forgiveness was great for them too.

There was no religious freedom in Sweden. The Lutheran church in Sweden was oppressive. You were not allowed to worship God in the way that you chose.

My great-great grandfather was fortunate enough to come to America after the great exodus of Swedes in the mid 1800s. The rest is history. My family from there on was able to make a simple, adequate living. My grandfather was a schoolteacher, his father a minister. My father was a minister. We always had enough and my parents taught me the value of giving and of having enough and that it didn't have to be more than that. They also taught me that racism is a sin.

My English ancestry goes back to some guy that baled out of the French army (he accidentally enlisted) and got a boat to America. Once in America, he joined Lincoln's army.

Most American Caucasians have similar backgrounds and stories. We were humiliated and degraded in many cases in Europe. We lived no better than slaves, even lived like slaves. In America, those people who ran the slave trade were the same people who had enslaved white people and who many Europeans were trying to separate from. The people who opposed slavery were people such as my ancestors who despised the ways of the old world.

We had a head start in America, though we too had humble beginnings. The African American beginnings were more difficult.

White people were the first in America to have the chance to reverse the evils of our original homeland. We didn't fully succeed. Our generational bondage has been deep and lasting. Our need for Christ's salvation is also evident. You were last. We had Christ before you. You were last, but the last shall be first.

Believe in the meaning of that passage and seize the Promised Land!

To order Rick Joyner's booklet call:
1-800-542-0278

Or write to:
Morning Star Publications
16000 Lancaster Highway

Charlotte, NC 28277-2061

Or go to: morningstarministries.org

Made in United States
Orlando, FL
27 September 2024